David Goggins

A biography

Author: Alia Bouta

ALIAREDA © 2023

In a world that values comfort and being like everyone else, there is a rough diamond whose life story shines through the pages of this biographical masterpiece. This book takes you on an amazing journey through the life and victories of a man who has defied the limits of the human mind and body.

book plan

Introduction

David Goggins, whose name is synonymous with grit, resilience, and unwavering determination, shows what it means to beat impossible odds. From growing up with an abusive father to becoming one of the toughest people on the planet, his story gives hope and inspiration to anyone who wants to break free from their past.

This fascinating biography goes into the darkest parts of Goggins' early life, when he had to deal with being overweight, being poor, and being treated badly because of his race. Even though he faced constant problems, he refused to give up. Instead, he used his problems as fuel to make a huge change in his life. After losing more than 100 pounds, the once-mocked and mocked person would push the limits of human endurance and become one of the most famous ultra-endurance athletes in the world.

This book peels back the layers of Goggins' unbreakable

spirit, showing how strong he was both physically and

mentally, as it tells the story of his lifelong quest for great-

ness. His story shows how strong mental toughness and

unwavering self-belief can be. He broke records as a Navy

SEAL and did things that seemed impossible in

ultramarathons and endurance challenges.

Aside from Goggins' physical achievements, this biography shows how he was able to inspire millions of people through his captivating public speaking and genuine openness. His goal in life has been to lift other people up and give them the tools they need to take control of their lives. This goal is felt deeply and profoundly on every page.

This book not only shines a light on the amazing things that one person has done, but it also teaches us a lot about the limitless potential that we all have. It makes us question the limits we put on ourselves and forces us to face the discomfort that comes with change and growth.

This book tells the story of a man who has changed what it means to be unbreakable. It is sure to keep you interested. Get ready for an adventure that will leave you inspired, motivated, and able to let go of the doubts that hold you back and live a life without limits.

1. Who is David Goggins?

David Goggins is a former Navy SEAL, ultramarathon runner, and motivational speaker. He is the best example of mental and physical strength. Goggins was born on February 17, 1975, in Buffalo, New York. He had a hard childhood, full of poverty, abuse, and racism.

Goggins has had a hard life since he was a child. His father left him, he was physically abused as a child, and he was constantly picked on because he is African-American. But his early problems lit a fire in him that made him more determined than ever to rise above the limits that bad luck had put on him.

Goggins wanted to change his life when he was 19, so he joined the United States Air Force Tactical Air Control Party. This gave him a big step forward in improving himself and finding out more about himself. After a few years of service, he joined the Basic Underwater Demolition/SEAL (BUD/S) program to become a Navy SEAL.

During BUD/S training, Goggins had to deal with many problems, such as long runs, swimming in the ocean, and not getting enough sleep. But he didn't give up. Instead, he pushed himself harder than he ever thought he could to overcome the obstacles in his way. After three tries, Goggins finally finished BUD/S training. He is now part of a small group of people who have been through one of the toughest military training programs.

After his time in the military, Goggins became an ultra-marathon runner and took on extreme endurance challenges as part of his job. He has finished a lot of races, like the Badwater Ultramarathon, which is 135 miles long and goes through Death Valley in very hot weather. Goggins has also finished multiple Ironman races and set the Guinness World Record for the most pull-ups done in 24 hours.

Goggins did a lot of amazing physical things, but that

wasn't enough for him. His strong will led him to dig deeper into self-discovery and tell others about how his journey changed him. Through his motivational speeches and his book "Can't Hurt Me," Goggins inspires people all over the world to embrace discomfort, break free from self-imposed limits, and reach their full potential.

Goggins is more than just a good athlete. He also shows resilience, mental toughness, and empathy. He uses his past experiences and successes to encourage people to get through hard times and try to grow as people. He is always reminding people that they are capable of much more than they think.

David Goggins' life story continues to inspire a lot of people and reminds us that we can overcome life's most difficult challenges if we work hard, never give up, and don't settle for average. He is a living example of the power of persistence and the ability of people to grow, which makes him a beacon of hope for people who want to change and get better.

2. The Beginnings of Resilience

David Goggins was born in Buffalo, New York, on February 17, 1975. From the moment he came into this world, it was clear that he was going to be great, even though he had a rough road ahead of him. David's early life experiences made him the extraordinary person he is today, known for his unwavering determination, mental toughness, and resilience.

David had to deal with a lot of hard things as a child that would have broken the spirit of most people. Born into a community that was divided by race, he often faced racism and being left alone. His early life was hard because he was poor and his family was always changing. His father, Trunnis Goggins Sr., had a hard time with drugs, which put a huge burden on young David. The problems he had at home and the many rejections and unfair things that happened to him at school made him into a young boy who was determined to rise above his situation.

David's early years were when he developed a strong will and a firm determination to reach his full potential. Jackie Goggins, his mother, did a lot to teach him the importance of working hard, not giving up, and being honest. She taught David the value of education and how important it was for him to be in charge of his own life. Even though Jackie didn't have much money, she made sure that her son had a safe and loving place to live where he could get through the problems he faced in the outside world.

Even though he had problems, David did well in school and always pushed himself to his limits. He learned that the cycle of mediocrity that was trying to swallow him up could only be broken through discipline and hard work. As a teenager, he started reading a lot. He looked for knowledge and wisdom in the pages of books, which would later help him grow as a person.

But the turning point in David's life was when he saw Army Rangers doing a hard training exercise on TV. That was the moment that would change the course of his life for good. He started to feel a strong need to push himself even further than what he had already done. David knew that joining the military would let him test his mental and physical limits and show himself and the world that he could do anything.

David set out on a hard journey to improve himself because he wanted to join the top ranks of the U.S. military. He stuck to a strict workout plan and pushed his body to the limit, breaking physical limits that seemed impossible to break. In the process, he turned himself into a powerful force, showing what the human spirit can do when it is driven by a strong will.

David Goggins had a hard childhood, but he didn't let that

make him who he was. He saw every problem as a chance to learn and grow, and each setback made him want to succeed even more. This part of his life set the stage for the amazing person he would grow up to be — someone who defies all limits and encourages others to do the same.

David had no idea that the toughness he learned as a child would become his greatest strength, taking him to heights he could never have imagined and making him an inspiration to millions of people around the world. This was just the beginning of his amazing journey. The next parts would test him even more, bringing him closer to being the best example of what a person can do.

3. The Unyielding Journey of David Goggins in College

David Goggins was about to start a new part of his life when he went to college. He set out on a journey that would test him physically, mentally, and emotionally. He had a strong will and a strong desire to succeed. He had no idea that this chapter of his life would be a turning point that would shape the person he would become.

David's first few months in college were not easy. He came from a hard background and had to deal with many problems that slowed his academic and personal growth. But he didn't let his situation make him who he was. He was determined to make a different future for himself, so he took advantage of every chance that came his way.

David went to college because he wanted to learn how to be more responsible and strong. David was determined to break out of the limits he had put on himself in the past, so he set big goals and worked hard to reach them. He learned the transformative power of pushing himself outside of his comfort zone by having to deal with the constant demands of his classes and by starting a strict fitness routine.

One day, David happened to read an article about ultrarunning, which is the hard sport of running longer distances than a typical marathon. He was interested in the idea, so he decided to accept the challenge and see how far he could go. Through training for many miles, he found a deep sense of purpose and untapped potential in himself that he didn't know he had. Ultrarunning became a metaphor for his life, which was full of pain and hard work that made him very determined.

David had some problems while he was in college. He had problems in school, with money, and in his personal life that would have made most people give up. But he didn't want to give up. He changed his approach after every setback, seeing failure as a chance to get better. He overcame these problems by working hard and staying focused. Each time, he came out of it stronger and more capable.

As David worked hard in college, he became an example for the people around him. His constant drive to improve himself inspired both his classmates and teachers. His story got around, and soon he was giving advice to other students and showing them that the only limits they had were the ones they put on themselves.

David's time in college was over, and he had done many things well and grown even more as a person. The student who had been having trouble was now an example of strength and determination. He left behind a legacy of strength and made a big difference in the lives of those who met him.

As David Goggins walked across the stage to get his college diploma, he knew that this was just the beginning of an amazing journey. The problems he faced in college helped him become successful in the future. They gave him a strong belief that anything is possible with the right attitude and hard work. David Goggins was ready to take on the world. His time in college had made him into an unstoppable force.

4. Triumphs and Transformations: David Goggins' University Career

Even though David Goggins had a hard childhood, he found peace and a sense of purpose in school in the early 1990s. He went to the University of Indiana with a strong will and a strong desire to grow as a person. There, he started a journey that would change his life and shape his future.

The change from high school to college was not easy for David Goggins. He didn't grow up with a lot of money, so he had to deal with financial problems that almost made him give up on his dreams. But his unquenchable thirst for knowledge drove him forward, and he refused to give up when things got hard.

Goggins realized right away that the discipline he had learned in the military would be key to his success in school. He was very determined to do well in school, so he set up a strict routine for studying. He spent a lot of time in libraries and stayed up late at night. After having trouble in school at first, he used every tool he could, like getting a tutor and starting study groups, to improve his knowledge.

Beyond his studies, Goggins understood how important it was to grow in all ways. He was very involved in clubs and organizations that were related to his interests and activities outside of school. Goggins thought that playing sports, joining debate clubs, and doing volunteer work were all ways for him to grow as a person and develop his character.

Goggins knew the value of working together and having a mentor while he was in college. He knew he could learn from people who were smarter and more skilled than he was, so he asked professors and other students for help.

He went into every situation with an open mind and built

relationships that not only helped him learn but also

helped him feel better when things were hard.

Goggins did not succeed at everything he tried in college.

Like any other student, he had to deal with failure,

disappointment, and setbacks. But Goggins didn't let his failures define him. Instead, he saw them as chances to grow. By learning from his mistakes, changing his plans, and keeping his strong will, he built up an unbreakable resilience that helped him move forward.

As Goggins' time in college was coming to an end, he thought about how much he had learned and done. Even though he had problems, he turned out to be a great student, both in school and in his personal growth. Graduation day showed how hard he had worked to be the best and how much he had changed during his time at the University of Indiana.

David Goggins' time in college helped him get ready for his future work. It gave him a thirst for knowledge, a strong work ethic, and the will to never give up. As he moved on to new things, he took the lessons he had learned in college with him and used them to help him deal with the challenges he would face on his amazing journey of self-discovery.

5. David Goggins - The Unbreakable Mindset

In this chapter, we will learn more about the amazing career of David Goggins, a man who has always pushed his physical and mental limits to do great things in his life. Goggins' life shows how strong determination and resilience can be. He overcame physical disabilities and fought his own demons to become a famous ultra-endurance athlete, motivational speaker, and author. This chapter will look at the key moments, accomplishments, and lessons he learned during his outstanding career.

David Goggins was born on February 17, 1975, in Buffalo, New York. From a young age, he had to deal with hard times. He grew up in an abusive home, where his father often hit him and called him names because of his race. Goggins had trouble learning, which made school hard and made him feel like he wasn't good enough. Even with all of these problems, he became mentally strong and worked hard to show the world what he was worth.

Goggins joined the U.S. Air Force when he was 19 years old. He was looking for a chance to grow as a person and a way to leave behind his troubled past. During his time in the military, he was part of a tactical air control party and earned many awards and learned many skills. After a few years, Goggins saw an opportunity to challenge himself even more. He joined the elite Navy SEALs and went through the notoriously difficult training program for SEALs.

Goggins fell in love with endurance sports after an injury

cut short his time as a Navy SEAL. He started running ultramarathons, triathlons, and Ironman races, where he often went up against the best athletes in the world. Even though Goggins didn't have much training or experience, he always pushed his body to the limit. This unbreakable spirit helped him finish races that others couldn't. People in the ultra-endurance community respected and admired him for how hard he worked to improve himself.

Goggins has done some amazing things that put him in the Guinness World Records, which is a very prestigious list. Notably, he did an amazing 4,030 pull-ups in 24 hours, which was the most of anyone. Goggins also won the Badwater Ultramarathon, which is known as the "world's toughest footrace." In scorching heat, he ran the 135-mile course, cementing his reputation as an endurance phenomenon.

Goggins became a sought-after motivational speaker when he realized that he had a special way of getting people excited and motivated. When he talks about how he overcame difficulties in his own life, he tells stories that are honest and compelling. Goggins also wrote the best-selling book "Can't Hurt Me: Master Your Mind and Defy the

Odds," in which he talks about the hard times in his life and gives advice on how to deal with problems, fear, and self-limiting thoughts.

Key Takeaways:

- David Goggins's professional life is defined by his unbreakable attitude, his ability to bounce back from setbacks, and his never-ending pursuit of personal excellence.

- Goggins has overcome physical and mental obstacles to become an amazing ultra-endurance athlete.

- He has set Guinness World Records, won extreme races, and inspired many people through his motivational speaking and writing.

- His story is a powerful reminder that we can all rise above our situations and change our lives through sheer determination and hard work.

David Goggins's professional life shows how strong the human spirit is. He has done amazing things against all odds because he was determined, disciplined, and always believed in himself. Goggins is an example for a lot of people who are facing their own problems. He shows them that with the right attitude, anything is possible. His story reminds us that no problem is too big to overcome, and that we have the power to change our own stories and reach our fullest potential.

6. United States Air Force Pararescue and the Indomitable Spirit of David Goggins

As the rescue team got ready for their mission, there was a lot of tension in the air. United States Air Force Pararescue (PJs) specialists were about to go on a mission they had never done before. They were known for their exceptional skills in providing medical aid and rescue operations in the most dangerous places.

Technical Sergeant David Goggins was in charge of this elite group. He was a great example of the unstoppable spirit and unwavering determination it takes to be a PJ. Goggins was known in the Air Force for having the strongest mind and body of anyone and for always trying to push the limits of human endurance. But his path to becoming a PJ and the problems he faced after that were nothing like what most people go through.

Goggins was born in Buffalo, New York, into a hard life, so he had to deal with a lot of problems from a young age. His early life was shaped by poverty, violence at home, and racism, which made him feel trapped and without hope. But Goggins refused to let his situation define him. Instead, he vowed to rise above his situation and make a better life for himself.

After a short time as an Airman in the U.S. Air Force, Goggins followed his dreams and went into the field of Pararescue. He was pushed to his limits and beyond by the tough selection process, which tested not only his physical skills but also his mental strength. As a PJ, Goggins realized that he had what it took to save lives and make a difference in the world.

Goggins looked at the PJ team behind him as he stood on the tarmac. Each member had earned their spot through hard training and experience in the real world, which made them a very strong unit. Goggins spoke to his team, and his fierce determination and unwavering commitment inspired them.

"Today, our mission isn't just to help people in trouble," he said, his voice carrying the weight of their shared goal. "It's also to show that the human spirit is unbreakable and that, no matter what, we can get through anything."

With those words, the team got on their plane and started their trip to a place nobody knew about. They had gone through a lot of training to get ready for the unknown, but nothing could have prepared them for what they would face on this mission. Their goal was to sneak into a remote area deep in territory controlled by the enemy and rescue a high-value target whose life was in danger. According to intelligence reports, the target, a captured intelligence officer, had been badly hurt and needed medical help right away.

As the PJ team got out of the plane and into the dark, Goggins led the way, his unwavering determination clear in every step. The darkness surrounded them, making them feel spooky and dangerous, but the PJs kept going with full concentration and unwavering courage.

The team sneaked up on the target while avoiding enemy patrols and getting through dangerous terrain. Goggins' ability to stay calm under a lot of pressure and quickly adjust to new situations was very helpful. He led his team through unexpected problems with ease.

When they finally got to the target, he was in a bad way. His wounds were bad, and he was running out of time. Goggins and his team didn't waste any time getting important medical help and stabilizing the situation. Even though there was a lot going on around them, the PJ team worked quickly and well because they were always professional and knew what they were doing.

But they still had a long way to go. As the enemy got closer, it became very important to leave. Goggins and his team planned a tactical retreat, fighting the enemy while making sure their patient was safe. Because they worked together and were skilled, they were able to hold off the enemy long enough for help to arrive.

Goggins looked back at what was happening on the battlefield as the rescue helicopter took them away. Even though the mission was a success, he knew that there were still a lot of people who needed their help. With a new fire of determination in his eyes, he vowed to keep going on his journey and never stop until everyone who needed help was saved. David Goggins's US Air Force Pararescue mission was just another part of a life he has spent serving others, not giving up, and pushing himself to the limit. His unwavering desire to be the best, his unbreakable spirit, and his amazing skills as a PJ saved lives and inspired many others to go beyond their own limits.

But David Goggins' story was far from over. It was a living example of the power of the human spirit and a never-ending source of inspiration for people who want to prove that anything is possible and overcome obstacles.

7. A Warrior Emerges - David Goggins in the United States Air Force Tactical Air Control Party

In 2001, David Goggins was at a turning point in his life.

After his first training in the U.S. Air Force, Goggins was

sent to the Tactical Air Control Party (TACP), which is one

of the most elite units in the military. He had no idea that his time in the TACP would help him become the tough warrior he is today.

Goggins was based at an airfield in the middle of the United States that was far away and had a feeling of being alone. The main job of the TACP was to work with ground units and give accurate and efficient command and control of air assets during combat operations. Goggins would have to deal with the harsh realities of war as a member of this highly specialized team.

From the first day, it was clear that the TACP required mental and physical toughness of the highest level. Goggins had to do a lot of hard training exercises that tested his stamina and pushed him to his limits. He had to carry a heavy pack, travel through dangerous terrain, and work out for long hours, all while keeping his mind sharp.

But that wasn't the end of it. Goggins was sent to the Middle East quickly, where he helped ground troops in the early stages of the war on terror. Every day, he had to deal with the heat and the constant threat of danger. Here, Goggins realized how important and heavy his job as a TACP operator really was. Goggins and his fellow TACP operators worked hard and risked their lives in dangerous combat zones to talk to different planes, coordinate airstrikes, and give important instructions to ground forces. Because of how important their job was, they had to be able to stay focused and change when things got tough.

Goggins's mental strength was put to the ultimate test during a particularly tough operation. Goggins had a hard time staying calm when he was pinned down by enemy fire and his fellow soldiers were counting on him. The chaos and fear almost made him lose control. But Goggins wouldn't give up. He had a never-say-die attitude that he had built up over his whole life.

Goggins became a source of calm in the midst of chaos because he was very disciplined and determined. He led friendly troops to safety and coordinated air support so well that it changed the course of the battle. This important event would cement his reputation as a warrior, both within the TACP and among his fellow soldiers.

But Goggins was never happy just to meet the standards set by his unit. He always tried to go above and beyond. He spent a lot of time improving his skills, getting certified in more advanced specialties within the TACP, and getting even more physically fit. Because he worked hard to be the best, his peers not only respected him but also saw him as a leader. Goggins's passion and determination were contagious, making those around him want to push themselves further and try to be great.

David Goggins' time in the United States Air Force Tactical Air Control Party was a crucible that made him the amazing person he is today. He learned what it meant to be strong, persistent, and self-disciplined by going through a lot of hard times in the military. These lessons would be the basis for his later successes and continue to inspire many people to find their own warrior spirit.

8. The Power of Giving: David Goggins' Extraordinary Acts of Charity

David Goggins is a well-known ultra-endurance athlete, Navy SEAL, and motivational speaker. He is known not only for pushing his own limits, but also for his heartfelt commitment to helping others. In this chapter, we look at Goggins' unique view on the power of giving and kindness through the extraordinary acts of charity he has done.

Goggins did not have an easy childhood. He was poor, he was bullied, and he was abused. These events gave him a strong sense of empathy and a desire to make a positive difference in the lives of others.

Goggins joined the Navy SEALs so he could serve his

country and develop a strong sense of duty and friendship with his teammates. His time in the military made him even more generous and taught him the importance of being selfless and helping others.

Goggins started his own non-profit organization because he saw how hard it was for veterans and their families. The goal of the foundation is to help veterans get back into civilian life by giving them resources and support in areas like mental health, education, and finding jobs.

Goggins has always used his love of endurance sports to raise money and bring attention to good causes. By running ultra-marathons and taking part in triathlons, he has inspired people to give money to groups that are working to solve problems like childhood cancer, poverty, and mental health issues.

Goggins believes that each person can make a difference, not just by giving money. He often talks to his fans on social media, giving them support and motivation when they are going through hard times and telling them to pay it forward. Goggins used his platform and influence to start philanthropy challenges that encouraged his fans and followers to do good things for others. By getting thousands of people to give back, he makes his own charitable work bigger and more effective.

Goggins shares his personal story and how acts of kindness and charity have changed his life when he gives motivational speeches. He gives people the tools they need to make a difference in the world, and he urges them to use their own abilities to do so.

David Goggins' amazing story of how he overcame trouble to become a force for good in the world shows how much charity can help both individuals and communities. His never-say-die attitude and commitment to helping others are a powerful reminder that we all have the power to make positive change, no matter what our circumstances are. By following Goggins's giving philosophy, we can reach our full potential to change people's lives and make a lasting difference in the world.

9. Pushing Beyond Limits - Marathon and Ultramarathon Running

David Goggins wasn't happy with just being a Navy SEAL and completing some of the hardest tasks ever seen by humans. He couldn't get enough of testing his stamina and mental strength, so he turned to marathon and ultramarathon running to keep pushing his body and mind to their limits.

As David started his journey to become a good marathon runner, he had to deal with a lot of problems. During his time in the military, he had serious injuries like stress fractures and broken bones. But he didn't let these setbacks define him. Instead, he used them to push himself to come back stronger. He saw running marathons as a way to go beyond what other people thought was possible.

David knew that in order to get ready for his first marathon, he would have to train and follow new rules. He had strict plans for every day, like getting up at 4 a.m. to run before the rest of the world was awake. He didn't just train to be physically strong; he also trained a lot to be mentally strong. David thought that the only way to be truly strong was to train both the mind and the body.

People know that marathons test people both physically and mentally. But David didn't let the pain stop him. Instead, it made him even more determined. He welcomed the pain because he knew that each step would make him stronger. During his first marathon, David learned a new level of mental toughness. He had to deal with blisters and push through muscle cramps.

Most people consider running a marathon a big accomplishment, but not David Goggins. He wanted to go even further, so he tried his hand at ultramarathons. In these races, the distances were longer than 50 miles, which pushed his endurance to levels he could not have imagined. David started training on dangerous terrains like mountains, deserts, and places with extreme weather. He looked for the hardest races in the world so he could really see how strong his body and mind were.

David's finish of the famous "Badwater 135" ultramarathon was one of his best ultramarathon achievements. It is 135 miles long and takes place in Death Valley, California, during the hottest part of the summer. It is known as the world's toughest foot race. David had to deal with blistered feet and temperatures over 120 degrees Fahrenheit. His body was pushed to its limits. Still, he kept moving forward and never doubted that he could get through this tough situation.

Ultramarathon running is a battle of the mind as well as the body. David learned to deal with the ups and downs that come with being so far away. He used mental tricks like visualizing, talking to himself in a positive way, and focusing on the present moment to resist the urge to give up. By keeping his mind in the present, he was able to block out the bad thoughts that would have stopped him from moving forward.

David found out what he was really capable of by running marathons and ultramarathons. Each race was a way to learn more about myself and find strength and resilience I didn't know I had. He realized that people only put limits on themselves in their minds, and it was up to each person to decide how far they were willing to go.

David Goggins's journey into marathon and ultramarathon running showed how hard he worked to be the best and how he could overcome challenges that seemed impossible to overcome. Running gave him a way to keep pushing his limits and find inspiration when things didn't go his way. With each step he took, David showed that anyone with unwavering determination and an unyielding spirit could do extraordinary things.

10. Recognitions and Decorations of David Goggins

David Goggins is an amazing person with a strong will. Throughout his career, he has not only broken a number of records, but he has also won a number of important awards and medals. In this chapter, we'll talk about the awards and honors he's received for his great work. These awards show that Goggins has a strong will and is determined to keep pushing himself.

Goggins' military career began when he was chosen to be a Navy SEAL for the United States. During his time in the SEAL teams, Goggins got a number of awards that showed how well he did and how much he cared about his job. Some of these are the Navy and Marine Corps Achievement Medal, the Navy Good Conduct Medal, and the Global War on Terrorism Expeditionary Medal. Even in his first few years of service, it was clear that Goggins was committed to doing his best.

Goggins never stopped trying to push the limits of his endurance. This led him to break several Guinness World Records. One of his most impressive achievements is running the most pull-ups in 24 hours, which he did in 2013 with a whopping 4,030 pull-ups. This showed how determined he was to beat expectations, and it made him known around the world as an athlete who broke records.

Goggins has done a lot of ultramarathons and endurance challenges in his career, which require an unimaginable amount of mental and physical strength. Because of how well he did in these events, the endurance community respects him and has given him several awards. Some of these awards are "Overall Winner" at the 2016 48-Hour National Championship race and "Completed 100 Miles" at different ultramarathons. These awards show how good Goggins is as an endurance athlete and how committed he is to pushing the limits of what people can do.

Many national organizations have taken notice of how hard Goggins works to be the best and how he can motivate others. His great accomplishments have been recognized by groups like the Endurance Society, which gave him the "Endurance Life Achievement Award." This award shows how much Goggins has changed the world of endurance sports.

Goggins has done amazing things with his body, but he has also become an inspiring speaker who has changed the lives of many people. His motivational speeches have helped him get a lot of attention, and the American

Communication Association gave him the "Outstanding Motivational Speaker" award. These awards show that Goggins can motivate and encourage other people to overcome their own problems.

David Goggins has won a lot of awards and recognition for his great work in many different areas, such as his military service, ultramarathons, and motivational speaking. These awards not only show how determined and persistent he is, but they also show how important he is to the endurance community and how much he inspires people all over the world. David Goggins's amazing journey shows how strong people can be, and his many awards and decorations show how much of an impact he has had on both physical and mental limits.

11. Unmasking the Ambitions: David Goggins' Personal Life

In this chapter, we learn more about David Goggins, a man with a strong mind and body who keeps his personal life secret. We want to learn more about what made Goggins the extraordinary person he is today, beyond the hard challenges and first-of-their-kind achievements that have come to define his public image.

David Goggins was born in Buffalo, New York, on February 17, 1975. His childhood was full of hard times and challenges, which pushed him to keep trying to grow as a person. Goggins grew up in a neighborhood where most of the people were white. He was treated unfairly and bullied because of his race, which changed who he is.

His troubled family life also had a big impact on how driven he was to do well. With a mother who beat him and a father who was rarely around, Goggins often found comfort in books, which helped him develop a strong imagination. But as he grew up, he realized how powerful it could be to use his bad experiences to help him reach his goals.

Goggins took a big step when he was 19 and joined the United States Air Force. This choice set him off on a journey that would change him in many ways. As a member of the Tactical Air Control Party (TACP), he found a new sense of purpose and a strong will to push past his physical and mental limits.

Goggins became one of the best soldiers in the U.S. Armed Forces after years of hard training and never giving up. He served in Iraq and Afghanistan more than once, showing a lot of courage and toughness in war zones. During this time, Goggins developed his strong will and unwavering attitude, which would later set him apart in a number of sports.

Goggins' physical skills became legendary, but health problems in his personal life caused him a lot of trouble. In 2005, he had major surgery to fix a birth defect in his heart. This life-threatening condition put Goggins's incredible strength to the test, and he had to face the fact that he might have to stop doing sports all of a sudden.

To the surprise of doctors and himself, Goggins not only got better, but he also did hard things that pushed the limits of what people could do. This chapter shows not only the physical problems he had to deal with, but also the emotional and mental strength that led to his amazing recovery.

Goggins knows that finding balance in his personal life is

just as important as his hard training and impressive phys-ical achievements. Even though he has done a lot of great things, he has often said that his all-consuming ambition and relentless pursuit of self-improvement make it hard for him to keep close relationships.

This chapter shows how hard it is for Goggins to make connections with people outside of his athletic activities. It looks at how he tries to find a balance between pushing his physical limits and taking care of his personal relationships. It also shows what he has had to give up along the way. David Goggins' life shows how important it is to be strong, determined, and always try to grow as a person. Goggins' life shows how each of us has the power to change. He had a hard childhood, but went on to have a decorated military career and do amazing things in sports. This chapter has peeled back the layers to show how one of the most respected and inspiring people in the world was shaped by his life experiences and the people around him.

12. David Goggins - Master Your Mind and Defy the Odds

In this chapter, we'll learn more about the amazing life of David Goggins, a person who has not only pushed the limits of physical accomplishments but also mastered his mind to do things that seem impossible. Goggins is widely thought to be one of the toughest men on the planet because he has been through a lot of hard times and kept going no matter what. His story is an example for everyone who wants to get past their own limits and reach their full potential.

David Goggins hasn't always been the unstoppable force he is now. Born in a small town in Indiana, he faced many problems as a child, including being abused and being overweight. As a young man working low-paying jobs, he was at the bottom of his life and desperate to make a change. At this point, Goggins set out on a journey to change himself and figure out what he was really capable of.

Goggins realized that in order to reach his goals, he had to get past the limits he had put on himself. He spent a lot of time studying the power of the human mind because the idea of mental resilience fascinated him. By working hard to improve himself, he came to believe that the mind can be the most powerful weapon against any kind of trouble. Goggins started a tough workout plan to deal with his weight and push himself beyond his physical limits. He tried extreme endurance races and military training programs, and along the way he had to deal with a lot of setbacks and failures. But by never giving up and finding new mental strength, he won many ultra-marathons and became a Navy SEAL, even though he was turned away from the program three times at first.

In the 4x4x48 challenge, Goggins ran 4 miles every 4 hours for a total of 48 hours. This is one of his most amazing accomplishments. This crazy endurance test showed how he was willing to put himself through pain and discomfort to reach his goals. He pushed his body to its limits and finished the challenge by sheer force of will. This made a lot of people realize the power of their own minds.

The Navy SEALs were not the end of Goggins' journey. He became a successful ultra-endurance athlete and even broke a few world records. He ran the "Badwater 135" race through Death Valley, which is considered the hardest footrace in the world. He is the only person to have finished the Navy SEALs' Hell Week, Army Ranger School, and Air Force Tactical Air Controller training.

Goggins is known as a motivational speaker and has written books that have sold a lot of copies. In his book "Can't Hurt Me," he tells his amazing story and stresses how important it is to control your mind if you want to be great.

Goggins has decided to spend the rest of his life getting other people to accept discomfort, push past their limits, and become the best version of themselves.

David Goggins' story shows how powerful the human mind is when it comes to overcoming problems and going against the odds. He has overcome a troubled past to become a role model for millions of people. He has done this by getting control of his mind and pushing his body to its limits. Goggins reminds us that we can be great if we work hard to improve ourselves and are willing to put up with the discomfort that comes with growth. As we continue on our journey, we must draw strength from his story and learn to use the power of our own minds to get past any obstacles that stand in our way.

13. Unleashing the Warrior Within - The David Goggins Story

In a world that often celebrates mediocrity and laziness, it's rare for someone to rise above their situation, challenging the status quo and pushing the limits of what people can do. David Goggins is one of these people. He is a living example of the strong will and determination that we all have.

David Goggins was born into a place where he was abused, didn't have enough money, and was treated badly because of his race. He faced impossible odds from the start. But in the end, it was his constant effort to get better and his refusal to settle for anything less than his best that would determine his fate.

In this chapter, we learn more about David Goggins's life and mind. We also learn what it really means to free your mind and win the war within. We look at what made him go from being a broken, overweight young man to a successful Navy SEAL, ultra-endurance athlete, and motivational speaker.

David's journey began with a turning point in his life: he

decided to break out of the limits he had put on himself and start a whole new way of life. He realized that he had let society's expectations and his own doubts control his choices up until that point, and he wanted a big change.

The first thing he did was face up to his physical limitations. David started a hard journey that required him to lose more than a hundred pounds and make his body work like a well-oiled machine. He relied on discipline and consistency, pushing himself through pain and exhaustion he couldn't even imagine. This helped him develop a strong sense of personal responsibility and ownership.

But the physical challenges were not the only thing that made David Goggins who he was. He knew that the only way to grow was to accept discomfort and problems in all parts of life. He looked for ways to test his mental and emotional strength, like running ultramarathons and going through SEAL training in the freezing cold.

David learned a lot about himself as he went along his journey. He realized how powerful it was to accept his weakness and use it as a tool to help him change. He got stronger and more resilient because he was honest about his weaknesses and learned from his mistakes.

"Calloused Mind, Fragile Body," David's motto, became a guiding principle in his life. He realized that even though the body could get weak and fail, the mind, if it was trained and prepared, would always win. He worked himself so hard that he was almost out of energy. This made him realize how much mental strength he had that he hadn't been using.

We learn about the lessons David Goggins wants to teach the world as we learn about his life and his quest for self-mastery. His life has taught him that everyone has a war-rior inside of them that is just waiting to come out. He tells us to use our hidden talents, to welcome discomfort and problems, and to always push ourselves past what we think are our limits.

David's story is a strong reminder that we are never really done with anything. There is always room for change, growth, and improvement. We can do great things with our minds if we have the discipline, resilience, and unwa-vering determination to win the war within.

In the next chapter, we'll look more closely at David Gog-gins's own ways of freeing the mind. We talk about the power of setting goals, visualizing them, and talking to yourself in a positive way. We also give readers tools and techniques they can use in their own lives.

Never Ending: Unshackle your mind and win the war within is not just a story about David Goggins. It is also a guide to finding your true potential, going beyond your limits, and becoming the best version of yourself. It's a look at the human spirit and a call to action for people who are ready to accept discomfort and reach great heights.

14. A Steadfast Journey

David Goggins was a young boy who grew up in a rural part of Indiana. From the time he was very young, he had to deal with problems. As Goggins went through a hard childhood filled with abuse and poverty, he slowly started to find the strength within himself that would fuel his amazing military career.

When Goggins joined the U.S. Air Force at the age of 19, he was quickly thrown into the demanding and structured world of military service. But he had to deal with a cruel problem: he was very heavy. The extra weight he carried was a big problem that stopped him from being successful. But Goggins, who never backs down from a challenge, didn't want to be limited by his body.

Goggins knew that if he wanted to join the military, he

would have to change a lot. He decided to lose 106 pounds in just three months, which was a big goal. Many people thought this was impossible, so it showed how determined he was.

Goggins pushed himself to his limits and beyond because he had a strong will and wouldn't give up. He did a lot of intense exercise and stuck to a strict diet, refusing to give in to the pains of hunger or tiredness. With every hard step, his mind got stronger, making him even more of a force to be reckoned with.

Goggins's hard work and desire to be the best quickly got the attention of his bosses. They saw that he was determined and wanted to do well, so they asked him to join the United States Navy SEALs training program.

As Goggins took on the hard and punishing SEAL

training, he once again pushed the limits of his physical and mental strength. He never let himself settle for average, and he took every chance to go above and beyond. But he knew that the path he had chosen would be hard.

Goggins faced the hardest tests of his life when he was hurt, couldn't sleep, and heard a voice inside him telling him to quit. But he didn't let pain or doubt stop him from getting to his goal. He was one of the few people to finish SEAL training because he worked hard, which added to his reputation as an unstoppable military force.

Goggins' time in the military didn't end with his SEAL training, though. He later became one of the first people to join the 75th Ranger Regiment of the US Army. Again, he took on the challenge and looked for ways to test himself and go beyond what was expected of him.

David Goggins's time in the military is a great example of how hard work and determination can pay off. From having a hard childhood to getting past big physical and mental obstacles, he shows that the human spirit has no limits.

Goggins is known today not only for what he did in the military, but also as a successful ultra-endurance athlete, motivational speaker, and best-selling author. His amazing journey through the military was the foundation for all of his later successes, and it has inspired a lot of people to accept their own hard times and use them as stepping stones to greatness.

In the next chapters, we'll look at David Goggins's life after he left the military. We'll talk about his accomplishments as a marathon runner, his work as a motivational speaker, and his huge impact on the people he meets.

15. Unleashing the Performance Beast - David Goggins' Journey as a Performance Athlete

People often say that David Goggins is the best example of

mental and physical toughness. He has done many great

things in the world of performance sports. Goggins'

journey as a performance athlete is nothing short of amazing. He has broken records in ultramarathons and finished the Navy SEAL Hell Week. This chapter looks at the problems he faced, the discipline he developed, and the way he thought in order to push his limits and change our ideas of what is possible for humans.

Goggins wanted to become a Navy SEAL when he was young. But at 300 pounds, being physically fit was hard for him in many ways. Goggins didn't let his limitations stop him from making a huge change. He trained hard and worked very hard to lose over a hundred pounds. Throughout his career as a performance athlete, he would keep coming back to this theme of determination.

Goggins is sure that the mind can handle much more than the body can. His philosophy is summed up in the "40% Rule," which says that when your mind says you are tired and can't go on, you are only at 40% capacity. Goggins keeps pushing himself past this limit, whether he's running ultramarathons, going through the hard SEAL training, or taking part in tough endurance races like the Badwater Ultramarathon.

One of the most important things about how Goggins does sports is that he is willing to embrace pain and discomfort. He doesn't try to avoid pain. Instead, he uses it to push himself forward. Goggins sees every challenge as a chance to grow and improve himself, whether it's enduring extreme physical exertion or getting past mental obstacles.

Goggins emphasizes the power of mental visualization in all of his training and races. He thinks that by picturing himself succeeding and going over different scenarios in his head, he can get ready for the challenges he will face. Goggins often imagines himself crossing the finish line or finishing the next hard task. This helps him stay focused and determined when he is tired or has doubts.

Goggins knows how important it is in performance sports to have a strong support system. Goggins knows that the people around him can help him get through tough times, whether it's the friendships he made during his SEAL training or the support and advice of his friends and family. He also loves the chance to be an inspiration to others, knowing that his successes can have a big impact on those around him.

In this chapter, we looked at David Goggins's journey as a high-performance athlete. Goggins is an inspiration in the world of sports because of how hard he works to be the best, how tough he is mentally, and how disciplined he is. Through his story, we've learned how important it is to set big goals, go beyond your limits, and be okay with being uncomfortable in order to perform at your best. David Goggins continues to motivate a lot of people to push their limits and find their inner potential.

16. The Indomitable Mindset of David Goggins

David Goggins is a living legend who has done amazing things with his body and mind. He used to be a Navy SEAL and is now a motivational speaker and an ultra-endurance athlete. But what really sets him apart is that he never gives up. In this chapter, we go deeper into Goggins's mind and look at the key ideas that have driven him to keep going after greatness. Through his story, we learn how to have a mindset that can help us overcome seemingly impossible problems and go far beyond what we think are our limits.

Goggins' life has been full of challenges, both inside and outside of him. But he never let his mistakes make him who he was. Instead, he made being tough a central part of his life. He knew that being resilient was not a skill to be learned, but a way of thinking that needed to be fed. Goggins tells us to be okay with being uncomfortable, to face our weaknesses head-on, and to see failures as steps on the way to success. By building up our ability to deal with problems, we can use them to help us grow as people.

Goggins thinks that mental toughness can be trained and built up like a muscle. He has been in many situations where his body and mind told him to stop, but he didn't give up. Through training and self-discipline, he has developed a strong, steady mind that lets him push through pain, fear, and self-doubt. Goggins teaches us that mental toughness is a choice we have to make every day — to embrace discomfort, to develop discipline, and to refuse to settle for mediocrity.

Goggins often talks about the 40% rule, which says that when we think we have reached our physical or mental limit, we have only used 40% of our true capacity. Goggins has broken his own records by following the 40% rule. He has finished many ultra-endurance races and hard physi-cal challenges. He challenges us to have a mindset of never giving up, to dig deep when everything is telling us to stop, and to go beyond what we think are our limits.

Goggins stresses how important it is to be responsible for our actions. He tells us how important it is to look at our-selves in the mirror and see our flaws, weaknesses, and ex-cuses. Goggins thinks that the first step to growth and im-provement is to be completely honest with yourself. By facing our flaws head-on and being honest about where we fall short, we can change into the people we want to be. The way we think is built on our sense of responsibility, which lets us take charge of our lives.

Goggins has always taken the path that isn't as popular. He thinks that we only grow and learn about ourselves when we leave our comfort zones. Goggins has been able to break out of the limits that other people and society put on him by challenging the norms and embracing the unusual. He tells us to change our ideas of what is possible, to be proud of who we are, and to follow our dreams no matter what other people think.

The way David Goggins thinks shows that we all have re-silience and limitless potential. By following his principles of resilience, mental toughness, and radical self-honesty, we can overcome any challenge and become great. Goggins' story reminds us that the most important battle is the one we have with ourselves. Once we win that battle, nothing can stop us. So, let's adopt David Goggins's never-say-die attitude and let our own potential soar to new heights.

17. David Goggins and the Iraq War

In this chapter, we look more closely at David Goggins's important role in the Iraq War. Goggins volunteered to serve in Iraq after he overcame many personal problems and found comfort in his military career. This chapter shows how hard he worked, how brave he was, and how much he cared about his fellow soldiers and the mission at hand.

Goggins was excited to be sent to Iraq after he finished his tough training and showed that he was an excellent soldier. In 2004, he finally got the news he had been waiting for, and a few weeks later, he was in the middle of the chaos of the war-torn country.

The Iraq War was known for its dangerous conditions, harsh terrain, and constant risk. Goggins quickly realized how bad the situation was after seeing how war destroyed both civilian lives and the lives of the soldiers stationed there. He never tried to hide from the harshness of his surroundings. Instead, he used it as motivation to work harder and do his best.

During his time in Iraq, Goggins was in a lot of dangerous situations. He and his fellow soldiers were in intense firefights and went on dangerous missions. His mental and physical toughness were always put to the test as he moved through dangerous areas, avoided enemy fire, and helped his team in important ways. Goggins was a big help to his team because he could stay calm under pressure and do his job well.

David Goggins found comfort and strength in the bonds he made with his fellow soldiers. Together, they won, went through hard times, and always looked out for each other. Goggins' time in Iraq was shaped by the friendships he made in battle, which led to friendships that will last a lifetime. Goggins also had to face personal demons that had been bothering him all his life while he was in Iraq. The war zone forced him to face his fears, doubts, and insecurities head-on. This gave him a unique chance to grow and change as a person. Goggins' unwavering determination and unbreakable spirit were made even stronger by his time in war.

As Goggins' time in Iraq came to an end, he took some time to think about what he had learned and how it had changed him. The war had taught him how important it was to be strong, flexible, and always committed to a cause bigger than oneself. These important lessons would shape the rest of his life and cement his reputation as a true warrior.

David Goggins's service in the Iraq War showed his unwavering dedication to duty, his amazing ability to keep going even when things were hard, and his unwavering loyalty to his fellow soldiers. He used the war zone as another place to test his mental and physical strength, which shows what a great person he was. When Goggins came back from Iraq, he was forever changed. He became a symbol of strength, courage, and the indestructible human spirit.

18. Conquering the Ultimate Challenge - Ultra-Marathons, Triathlons, and Ultra-Triathlon

David Goggins had already pushed himself to his limits many times, but he was about to face his hardest test yet: a series of ultra-marathons, triathlons, and the ultra-triathlon, the final and most difficult challenge. He knew that this trip would be different from all the others, and that he would have to use even more of his mental and physical strength.

The first thing on his schedule was an ultra-marathon, which is a scary 100-mile race through rough terrain. Goggins had always been a strong runner, but he had never tried to run this far before. As he stood on the starting line, he thought of his motto: "When you think you're done, you're only at 40%. "Keep going!" He pushed through the pain with every step, finding the strength to keep going even when his body begged him to stop.

Goggins felt both tired and excited as the finish line of the ultra-marathon got closer. When he ran through the tape, he knew he had passed another important step on his way to becoming the best version of himself. But he also knew that he still had a long way to go.

The next thing on his list was a series of triathlons, which involve swimming, cycling, and running. Goggins had trained hard in each event, never losing his focus or determination. He pushed himself to the limit with every stroke, pedal, and step, willing his body to go faster, farther, and stronger.

His endurance was tested in different ways by the triathlons, which forced him to adapt to the different needs of each leg. When he was swimming, he had to fight against rough water, strong currents, and his own fears. As the miles went by, he rode his bike through dangerous terrain and fought off fatigue. In the end, he had to use all of his strength and mental toughness to keep putting one foot in front of the other while running.

But when most athletes would have thought their journey was over, Goggins knew he still had one more challenge to face: the ultra-triathlon. This toughest test ever combined the long distances of an ultra-marathon with the constant endurance needed for a triathlon. He would have to swim, ride a bike, and run for days on end, even though he was not getting enough sleep, was very tired, and was fighting his own mental demons.

Goggins knew that he would have to give everything he had to this final challenge. He set out on his multi-day trip after carefully planning and being very disciplined. Physically, he was ready because of his training, but his mental toughness would be the key to his success.

Days became nights, and nights became days, but Goggins kept going, pushing his body and mind past what they thought were their limits. He found comfort in the bad times by letting himself feel the pain and turning it into energy that drove him forward. He knew he could never give up, because his journey wasn't just about the races; it was also about showing himself and others that the human spirit is limitless.

When Goggins finally crossed the finish line of the ultra-triathlon, he was so tired and happy that he just fell over. He had pushed his body and mind to the limit, facing physical and mental challenges that were unimaginable. But he overcame them one by one, showing that anything is possible if you have enough guts, determination, and faith in yourself.

David Goggins' journey took a big turn in Chapter 7. It showed how strong-willed he was and showed that people have limitless potential. When he thought about all the hard things he had been through, he knew that his journey was far from over. With a renewed sense of purpose and an insatiable desire for more growth, Goggins promised to keep pushing himself, encouraging others to do the same, and forever raising the bar for what is possible in the world of endurance sports.

"Can't Hurt Me: Master Your Mind and Defy the Odds" is an autobiography written by ultra-marathon runner and former US Army Special Forces member David Goggins.

The book tells the story of Goggins's amazing journey, including how he overcame many challenges and pushed his mental and physical limits to become one of the best athletes of his time.

Goggins talks about his hard childhood, which was full of violence and abuse, and how he was able to break out of this cycle by using his mental strength. He then talks about how he joined the Navy SEALs, which are the special forces of the US Navy, and how he had to go through cruel training to join this elite group. Goggins never gave up and reached his goal, even though he had many failures and problems along the way.

The book focuses on the advice and life lessons that Goggins learned on his journey, especially about discipline, mental toughness, and pushing oneself to the limit. He tells people to push their limits and not let fear or doubt lead them. Instead, he tells them to learn how to control their minds so they can get over their weaknesses and reach their goals.

"Can't Hurt Me: Master Your Mind and Defy the Odds" is both an inspiring story of a personal victory and a useful guide for people who want to change their way of thinking and go beyond their own limits. It tells readers to get out of their comfort zones and try something new, and it shows how willpower and determination can make the impossible possible.

19. The Unbreakable Net Worth of David Goggins

David Goggins is a great example of a person who never gives up and has a strong mind. He is one of the most remarkable people in the world. David Goggins has done amazing things with his body and mind, but he has also built up a large net worth that shows how hard he has worked to be the best in many areas. This chapter goes into detail about the things that make up David Goggins' net worth. It looks at the different ways he makes money and how his wealth has changed his life and mission.

David Goggins did not have an easy road to financial

success. Growing up in a tough place with a lot of poverty and hardship, he had to deal with a lot of problems that would have stopped most people. David grew up in a broken home and had to deal with a violent father. These things taught him the value of being strong and able to rely on himself. These deeply rooted traits would later play a big role in how he thought about money and success.

David Goggins's decision to join the military was a big turning point in his life. As a Navy SEAL and later in the U.S. Air Force Tactical Air Control Party, Goggins worked on his mental and physical discipline and learned how to push past what people thought were their limits. Even though his time in the military may not directly add to his net worth, it sets the stage for his later successes and helps him build a reputation that brings him money-making opportunities.

After leaving the military, David Goggins started a new chapter as an ultra-endurance athlete, where his incredible feats became the stuff of legend. Goggins broke records and pushed the limits of human endurance by doing things like running ultra-marathons, cycling long distances, and completing hard challenges like the Badwater 135 and the HURT 100. These amazing things made him famous all over the world and helped him get a lot of sponsorship deals, money from elite races, and speaking gigs that add a lot to his net worth.

David Goggins is a great athlete, but he also has a unique ability to inspire and motivate others. Realizing this, he used his amazing life experiences to write two best-selling books, "Can't Hurt Me" and "Living with a SEAL." Both books tell the story of his journey from trouble to success, which teaches us a lot about the power of staying strong.

Goggins has become a highly sought-after motivational speaker because of how well his books have done and how interesting he is when he speaks. He charges high fees for his speeches, which has helped him make a lot more money.

Big brands want to be associated with David Goggins's inspiring image because he is so determined and has a magnetic personality. Goggins has signed lucrative endorsement deals with well-known companies that make everything from athletic gear to health supplements. These partnerships give him money and let him promote products he really believes in, which raises his net worth even more.

David Goggins's financial success has changed his own life, but he also works hard to make a positive difference in the lives of others. His charitable work includes raising money for military veterans, giving money to charities that raise awareness about mental health, and giving motivational speeches to thousands of people. Even though these things may not have a direct effect on his net worth, they are building a legacy of kindness and change that will surely be more important than any amount of money.

David Goggins has built a net worth that shows how hard he works to be the best and how committed he is to his own growth. From his humble beginnings to his amazing achievements as an athlete, author, speaker, and philanthropist, Goggins' net worth shows the power of resilience, determination, and being able to turn adversity into success. David Goggins's financial success continues to inspire, empower, and change people's lives all over the world. This shows that true wealth is much more than just material possessions.

Conclusion

In the end, David Goggins's biography is a deep and inspiring story about a person who went against all odds to become one of the most famous and respected athletes and motivational speakers of our time. Goggins shows the power of sheer will and unwavering commitment in the way he works hard to improve himself and overcomes both physical and mental challenges.

From his troubled childhood to becoming a Navy SEAL, ultra-endurance athlete, and world record holder, his story shows that we all have limitless potential and challenges us to go beyond our perceived limits and use discomfort as a stepping stone to greatness. David Goggins shows that the only real limits we have in life are the ones we put on ourselves by never giving up on self-improvement and never giving up on himself. This biography is an inspiring journey that will make readers want to take on challenges, keep going after their dreams, and, in the end, live a life without regrets.

Made in the USA
Las Vegas, NV
13 December 2023

82747006R00059